THE READER-VIEWER-LISTENER

An Essay in Communication

by Lester Asheim

LIBRARY OF CONGRESS
WASHINGTON
1987

THE CENTER FOR THE BOOK

Viewpoint Series, no. 18

Library of Congress Cataloging-in-Publication Data

Asheim, Lester Eugene, 1914 –
The reader-viewer-listener.

(The Center for the Book viewpoint series ; no. 18)
Bibliography: p.
1. Books and reading. 2. Communication. I. Title.
II. Series: Center for the Book viewpoint series ; 18.
Z1003.A77 1987 028'.9 87-4144
ISBN 0-8444-0550-7

The paper used in this publication meets the requirements for permanence established by the American National Standard for Information Sciences "Permanence of Paper for Printed Library Materials" (ANSI Z39.48-1984).

Illustrations by Rudolph Ruzicka

Foreword

THE CENTER FOR THE BOOK IN THE LIBRARY OF CONgress was established by law in 1977. In explaining to Congress why he felt the center was needed, Librarian of Congress Daniel J. Boorstin emphasized the need in today's society to explore and extend the relationship between books and other media: "We must see that the book is the useful, illuminating servant of all other technologies, and that all other technologies become the effective, illuminating acolytes of the book."

In this essay, Center for the Book adviser Lester Asheim explores books and their relationship to other media in an even wider context, examining books and reading as a part of the total communication process. Readers, he points out, are also viewers and listeners. It is the active involvement of the reader-viewer-listener that intrigues Asheim and leads him to suggest that "the meaning of communication rests as much with the person who receives the message as it does with the person who originally formulated it." And what of the book? Asheim sees it as essential to our lives as "the medium most capable of adapting effectively to the greatest number of different needs." Our natural inclination to honor the book must not, however, divert our attention from other essential means of communication.

The purpose of the Center for the Book is to stimulate public interest in books and reading and to encourage the interdisciplinary study of books and the printed word. Its symposia, lectures, projects, and publications are supported by private contributions from individuals and corporations. For further information, write The Center for the Book, Library of Congress, Washington, D.C. 20540.

JOHN Y. COLE
Director
The Center for the Book

A distinguished librarian, Lester Asheim is professor emeritus of library science at the University of North Carolina at Chapel Hill. Before going to Chapel Hill in 1975 he taught at the University of Chicago Graduate Library School (where he served as dean from 1952 to 1961) and served as director of the American Library Association's International Relations Office (1961-66) and the ALA Office for Library Education (1966-71).

THE READER · VIEWER · LISTENER

WHEN PATRICIA AND GORDON SABINE SET OUT TO DO their study *Books That Made the Difference,*[1] they quite deliberately and purposefully limited their attention to the act of reading and to a single carrier of the reading experience. The success of their broad-based personal interview survey suggests that similar explorations of other communication experiences besides that of the book would be equally rewarding, if we are to understand the full reality of how people's lives are influenced by contact with the ideas of others. The Center for the Book, despite its focused appellation, has been interested all along in the broader range of communication experiences, of which book reading is only one.

The special experience of book reading, however, is complicated enough in itself. What comes out of the Sabines' study is its overwhelming evidence of how unpredictable and how varied the influence of book reading is. The list of titles cited by the respondents is an interesting aspect of the study, but it could not be used as an infallible list of influential readings for others. What the responses clearly indicate is that a reading experience is an individual matter; that what opens the eyes of Reader A in wonder and revelation might well cause the eyes of Reader B to droop in boredom and indifference. What is most revealing about the study is not primarily the identification of specific books that have had an influence, but the fact of influence itself. How does it work? What happens in those instances when, through the manipulation of certain symbols, an impact occurs that makes a difference in the lives of some of the people who were exposed to that particular ordering of black marks on white paper? The same question could be raised about any other arrangement of symbols that are capable of conveying ideas, stimulating emotions, and altering how and what we think.

The Symbol and the Thing

IF IT IS THE MANIPULATION OF SYMBOLS THAT CARRIES the message — and not simply the paper and boards in which it appears — then we should take the Sabines' title as a figurative rather than a literal statement of the phenomenon they are addressing. It is not the *book* that made the difference in most cases, but the ideas that the book contained. If anything, the book is most likely to make a difference *as a book* when reading is not involved. As an example, a child might place an unabridged dictionary on a chair in order to use its height and solidarity to make it possible to reach a forbidden cookie jar on a high shelf. But even in this example, I have resorted to something of the same kind of synecdochic usage as that of the Sabines. The reward of that inventive, instrumental use of the book is not the cookie jar, but the cookie inside. Like a book, the cookie jar is a carrier of the reward; it is not the reward itself. In the Sabine study, the book as artifact, rather than as a carrier of ideas, is not the focus.[2]

The reason that the Sabines chose to study the influence of the book, rather than the influence of communication in general, is that historically the book has been the most effective carrier of ideas and information that can alter the lives of those who come into contact with them. But it is not and never has been the only one. Actual speech, through direct contact with another human being, is much more frequently the medium through which people are introduced to the ideas of others. The book is simply a device for preserving words, and for making connection possible with those humans-with-ideas with whom we do not have direct contact.

In many instances, the impact that is credited to a book — the books that have changed our minds, the books that have shaped the modern world—has actually come from interpreters who have intervened between us and those seminal works. It is true that the lives of many of us living today have been shaped by Adam Smith, Darwin, Marx, Freud, and other such influential writers, but even when we have absorbed their ideas into our own thinking, and are able to use their very words as our own ("laissez-faire," "survival of the fittest," "Oedipus complex"), we need not have learned those words or concepts through our own reading of their originators. Teachers, commentators, popularizers, lecturers, and, of course, writers of other books based upon the "influential" works are the ones who have spread the word, and they have been the more direct sources of our knowledge in most cases. Even the Bible (perhaps the single most influential book of all in the Western world) is known to us through interpreters — priests, ministers, rabbis, teachers, and evangelists — as much as it is through our own direct reading of The Book itself.

This phenomenon of the role of mediators who often diffuse ideas more widely than do their originators was first brought to the attention of modern researchers in communication effects when a study of voting behavior discovered, almost by inadvertence, that a great number of the respondents decided how they would vote after talking it over with a friend or acquaintance rather than from their newspaper reading or their radio listening, or even from directly hearing the exhortations of the candidates.[3] This discovery — of the importance of personal influence and the role of "opinion leaders" in spreading the word — added an important dimension to communication study. This phenomenon developed into a theory called, at first, "The 2-Step Flow of Information," and, later, as its greater complexity became apparent, "The N-Step Flow of Information."

I should like to suggest that the familiar phrase "spreading the word" is far too restrictive. The word, which is itself only a symbol standing for a unit of meaning, is not the only form through which ideas may be transmitted. Music, painting, sculpture, choreography, pantomime, and even the shapes and colors of objects (traffic signs, for example), are extremely effective, wordless codes to those who understand how to decipher them. And when we do not know the meaning of the symbols well enough to break the initial code—as in musical or choreographic notation, for example — the performing arts themselves provide interpreters: actors, dancers, musicians who translate the message for us. Even where we can decode the printed symbols, as in Shakespeare, an interpreter can enrich the experience. The translation of the literary form from dramatic literature to theatrical performance often opens up depths of feeling we might never have plumbed through our own reading of the verbal text itself. The interpreters impose an additional code of their own to supplement, or even replace, the original form of the message as formulated by the original communicator.

Think what a complex set of wheels within wheels is involved in communication through the performing arts. The stage production of a printed text adds costumes, settings, lighting, music, gestures, and mime which are an additional set of symbolic presentations to be deciphered and form part of the total experience we bring away from a theatrical performance. Films add their own set of communicative devices. Since the advent of "talking pictures," for example, it is almost unthinkable to have a film without a musical score to manipulate our mood and to alert us to specific moments of key action. The ubiquitous musical background has become so much a part of our expectation, that a sudden cessation of the music can itself carry a dramatic impact: the absence of an expected message becomes a message in its own right (as Sherlock Holmes reminded us could happen, in *The Hound of the Baskervilles*). But then, silences—pauses—have long been a part of oral messages, symbolized on the page by commas, dashes, semicolons, and alterations in spacing. Similarly, camera angles, close-ups, tilted camera, flashbacks, and many other nonverbal communication devices have been part of the message of which many filmgoers are not consciously aware but by which they are moved nevertheless.

We are often unmindful of the fact that we have learned how to interpret, through experience, the many different symbolic forms of expression that convey meaning to us. We recognize in a general way that we must know the language in order to interpret a speech, and must master reading skills in order to interpret print. We are not always aware that the many nonverbal forms of communication are "languages" too. As receivers of messages in any of the several forms of communication available to us, we must master the special skills and capabilities without which those messages cannot make the difference in our lives.

The Role of the Receiver

IT IS THIS ACTIVE INVOLVEMENT OF THE READER-viewer-listener in the total communication process that I find so fascinating. It suggests that the meaning of communications rests as much with the person who receives the message as it does with the person who originally formulated it, and that without a receiver, a message is — to all intents and purposes — not yet a message.

This seems obvious enough, yet the active role played by the receiver of messages — whether the message is carried in print or through one of the many other communication devices that exist in our society — has not always been given much attention by those who studied the communication process. When Shannon and Weaver formulated their now familiar model of communication, their attention was placed primarily on the technology.[4] As telephonic engineers, they were interested in the phenomenon of literal "noise on the channel" which interferes with the clear reception of the message *as sent*. For their purposes, the meaning of the message as such, and its effect upon the receiver, were outside their concern. If the telephone line could distinguish clearly between the sounds of *m* and *n*, for example, and did not fade before the transmission was completed, it was considered to be an efficient carrier. To test that kind of efficiency, nonsense syllables would do; but in communication between human beings, nonsense syllables introduce a different kind of noise, well within the meaning of that term (i.e., interference with reception of the message). In Shannon and Weaver's context, the sender of the message is more important than the receiver of it; effective communication is said to be achieved if the same words that were put into the channel come out clearly at the receiving end. What is made of those words by the receiver is not part of the model. In this approach to communication study, the mind of the receiver is a tabula rasa, not an equal participant in the transaction.

Later, when Harold Lasswell restated the communication model in social science terms, he personalized it: Who (the Sender) says What (the Message) through which Channel (the Medium) to Whom (the Receiver)?[5] And then he added the element that is the subject of this essay: "With What Effect?" This question, which is concerned not just with the mechanical operation but with its social consequences, adds a new dimension—the dimension explored by the Sabines. And when we move into this realm where human beings are involved, we are inevitably drawn into considerations that call upon the humanities as well as the social sciences and technology. Having identified the channel that carries the message, we are faced with the challenge of examining how the channel is used, which soon brings us to an examination of not only the matter of the message but the manner of its presentation, as an element that makes one message more effective than another, even when both are sent via the same medium, concerned with the same subject, and intended for the same receiver.

It is important, obviously, to make sure that the message is not garbled in its transmission, but simply to establish letter-by-letter accuracy is not enough. "Something there is that doesn't love a mall" makes good American sense in the last quarter of the twentieth century, and it probably wouldn't be caught by the spelling-correction feature on your home word-processor. We need the total context to be able to detect the error in transmission. But after we have changed the *m* to a *w*, we are still faced with another intriguing question about the affective power of these symbols. Why "Something there is," instead of "There is something?" What difference does it make? Why does it make a difference? And (the importance of the receiver), to whom?

It is upon the alertness to such subtle shadings as this that a great deal of the most effective communication rests, for those who are sufficiently fine-tuned to be affected by the distinction. And it is this recognition — of the role played by the receiver as something more than a target hit by the sender of the message — that began to challenge the "Bullet" theory of communication effectiveness (a view still widely held by those who would censor), and suggested instead that our concern is certainly as much with what the receiver does with the message as it is with what the message does to the receiver.

And here we come to a key aspect of a communication's effectiveness: The degree to which the individual receiver of the message possesses that necessary capacity for fine-tuning. This factor cannot be measured by total sales figures, or Nielsen ratings, or the speed with which multiple messages can be transmitted. This is not to say that mass appeals and individual effectiveness are necessarily mutually exclusive or unrelated. Many of the books that made a difference in the Sabine survey were best-sellers, and the fact that "everybody" was reading them may well have been what led the respondents to them in the first place. But each person reads, even a best-seller, alone; even the messages that go out simultaneously to mass audiences across the country are not always received in a mass situation, but by an individual. Within the context of the Sabine study, therefore, a particular reading, mentioned only once, was considered just as important as a title mentioned frequently. If some books were mentioned by more than one person, that was an interesting datum, but what was even more interesting was the fact that in most such cases the same book turned out to be effective in entirely different ways for each reader of it. When we begin to examine why that should be so, we inevitably find that the person who receives the message is the key variable, even when that receiver is not conscious of his or her active participation in a communication transaction.

The most easily measured aspects of communication activities may not therefore be their most important aspect when we care about the transfer of ideas. On the other hand, there are some basic and obvious conditions that must be met. At the start, it is clear that the message cannot be assimilated if the receiver does not know the code in which it is formulated. It is widely recognized that one must know how to read in order to be reached by print, and the current concern over adult illiteracy reflects this knowledge. The same proviso must be made for any other form of communication, and our popular usages reflect this too: terms like "computer literacy" or "film literacy" may disturb the purist, but they are simply a recognition that the *ability to use and interpret the symbols which transmit meaning* is essential to the understanding of messages, however they are transmitted. We pay less attention than we should to the fact that every communication, in whatever format, is an encoded message. We tend to imagine, for example, that anyone can watch a film, or a television program, and understand its meaning without any previous introduction to the medium. It may be true that the decoding of the symbols is more readily mastered at the basic level for television than it is for the deciphering of print, but even television has its conventions that must be learned before it begins fully to convey the messages it carries. Studies have shown that these conventions can be grasped at an age far below that required for attaining reading ability, and we have all seen how preschool children, and even the family dog and cat, soon learn the skill of TV viewing, recognizing which patterns of dots represent human beings, no longer confused when a character's image walks out of the frame, and able to distinguish the commercial from the story itself. Nevertheless, that reaction is a learned one; until the convention is accepted, the flicker of light is meaningless, and the format is confusing. People doing fieldwork in primitive societies once assumed that the language barrier could readily be eliminated simply by showing an educational film, but they discovered that even adults, if they had never seen a film, had to learn how to interpret a simple picture of a familiar object. The "language" of visual presentation was a lesser barrier than verbal language, but it was a barrier nevertheless. When you move to a more complex work of filmic art, there are many, many messages lost to the viewer who has not learned how to interpret the meaning intended by the cut, the fade-out, the close-up, the traveling shot, the conventions of theatrical pantomime, and so on. In other words, "Do you read me?" is a question that no longer refers only to the decoding of words on paper. We now recognize — without paying much attention to our knowledge — that a life-or-death message ("One if by land and two if by sea") can be conveyed in full even to someone who is unlettered, but only if there is agreement between sender and receiver about the meaning of the code.

The Meaning of Literacy

ALL TOO OFTEN, TOO, WE FORGET THAT IN ANY KIND OF communication setting "literacy" can exist at many different levels. One can be literate by official definition, and still not be able to ferret out the meaning of many forms of prose presentation. The term "functional illiteracy" takes cognizance of this at a fairly low level, but there are differences in the ability to interpret that can occur even among those who are highly literate as well. A person who has no trouble with Faulkner may be completely baffled by presumably simple do-it-yourself instructions; professors who sail through Wittgenstein have to call on an auto mechanic (who may have been a high school drop-out) for guidance through their automobile manuals. This is not only a matter of vocabulary; it is tied to a way of thinking, an acceptance of conventions of the form, and a mind-set. As Will Rogers put it, "Everybody is ignorant, only on different subjects," and the several forms of communication represent "subjects" about which we possess different degrees of ignorance.

The conventions of the form are important. Coleridge refers to "that willing suspension of disbelief . . . which constitutes poetic faith," referring to the cooperation of the reader with the writer that is achieved in part through a familiarity with the conventions of the form. We have to learn to understand the meaning of certain conventions in poetry that differ from those in prose; in theater, conventions different from those in film; in mime and dance, conventions different from those in the lecture hall; and in line and shape and pictured symbols, conventions different from noun and verb and adjective. And where, in any of these formats, new experiments are initiated and new relationships are introduced — between word and gesture, line and shape, notes on the scale, soft and sharp focus — an adjustment is required even for those familiar with the standard vocabulary of the medium.

This sometimes means that those who are truly familiar with the tradition find it hard to accept the introduction of innovation because it departs from their expectations. Not so long ago, many habitual concertgoers could not hear anything that resembled music in the works of Stravinsky, and museum visitors could not tell what the subject was of an Impressionist painting. They were tied to a different set of conventions, and their high degree of literacy in that set made it harder for them to understand messages that departed from it. "A picture is supposed to look like something" is a very limiting preconception; it is very like the resistance to fiction by many readers whose preconception is that there is no point in spending time reading what is "not true." The underlying question — "What is Truth?" — is an old one, and in the interests of bringing this essay to its conclusion, I too will not stay for an answer.

On the other hand, the real significance and impact of a departure from the convention is often only fully appreciated by those who know the convention and recognize what is happening. The pleasure one can derive from surprise and experimentation depends to a very large degree on the knowledge of the traditional rules and the challenge represented by departure from them. It is often difficult for a later generation to understand why a work of art such as *Nude Descending a Staircase, Rhapsody in Blue,* or *Ulysses* created such a sensation when it first appeared. In the interim, the novelty has been assimilated into the canon: the once-new has become old-hat.

It can work both ways: the devotee of Palestrina can hear no music in Punk, while the Heavy Metal addict thinks a Haydn symphony is just a bunch of meaningless noise. Beauty does lie in the eye of the beholder and the ear of the listener, but other qualities are required over and above the basic knowledge of the code alone. There is a difference between being able to identify each individual letter or musical note and appreciating the shape and form of the total work made up by a succession of those letters or notes in a variety of combinations. Understanding is more complex than simple recognition.

One of the important aspects of exposure to any medium, then, is the fact that it is a learning process in the language of the medium itself. Only through repeated experience with a medium does one begin to understand its conventions and recognize variations in their use. The more one is exposed to a particular medium, the more one begins to appreciate its capacity to convey additional levels of meaning, and to comprehend not only the literal message but the nuances that are embedded in its manner of presentation. A multileveled experience begins to come through and — as in reading — one begins to respond to the way in which the medium is used as much as to the dictionary meaning of the words and the conventional features of its grammar. Something there is that touches us more deeply because of the order of the words, over and above the words as such.

That is why the promotion of reading ("Read More About It!") is so essential in a society that offers so many other formats of communication. Without a familiarity with the particular form and its capabilities, the mere performance of the act (of reading as well as of listening or viewing) is bereft of much of its power to move and excite and enlighten. And that is why, too, in so many reports on the effects of a particular reading, we find that a major effect of the reading was to lead to more reading; in addition to learning something about the subject matter of the reading, the reader has also learned something about the power of reading itself.

Most forms of communication build upon the assumption that the receiver of the message over a particular channel is familiar with both the content and the style of that channel. Literary allusions enrich the printed text — for the reader who recognizes the source of the allusion. Radio and television are more likely to make their allusions to other broadcast programs and characters; films not only quote lines of dialogue from other films but also imitate particular filmic devices that touch a chord in the knowledgeable filmgoer. And certain genres, like parody or burlesque, rest almost exclusively for their effectiveness on the audience's prior knowledge of the lampooned work.

The value of continued exposure, then, cannot be overlooked. There is a story — perhaps apocryphal — about Walter Damrosch, who introduced a new and experimental work at a symphony concert. Upon its completion, the sounds of displeasure far exceeded the applause. When quiet was restored, Damrosch acknowledged the audience's reaction as follows: "You did not like this work? Very well, we'll play it again."

He was right, of course. Listening is as much a form of learning as reading, and if you don't get the meaning at the first exposure, try, try again. Those who are unwilling to try again all too often avoid further contact with any messages over a similar channel. While I have never accepted the literal purport of McLuhan's "The medium is the message," I must acknowledge that in practice it is frequently true that people base their expectation about a medium upon a few sample messages it may have carried, and as a result of that limited experience do not — or cannot — or will not — accept any other messages it is capable of transmitting. Once again, the receiver determines — often in advance — whether there will be reception of the message, quite apart from the nature of the specific message itself. The mind-set of the receiver can be "the noise on the channel" as great as any static interference in the process of transmission.

An interesting example of how one's mind-set alters the interpretation of the message is given by Andrew Greeley in an introduction he has written for a recent printing of Douglas's *The Robe*. To Greeley, coming upon the novel as a young reader, the influence was enormous and lasting.

> It changed my mind about religion, about fiction, and about the possible relationship between the two. . . . Finally, almost forty years later, when I turned to storytelling of my own, it was a result of a long intellectual and imaginative process that had started with reading "The Robe."[6]

On the other hand, he reports that the official Catholic press found it to be a dangerous and unacceptable work for its "naturalist" and "rationalist" approach and denounced it, fearing its influence on the minds of its readers. Greeley's enthusiasm is for the *art* of the book; the official Catholic concern at the time was over its *ideas*. Contrast these approaches with that of Edmund Wilson, who found in *The Robe* neither art nor ideas:

> It is so difficult, when one first glances into *The Robe,* to imagine how any literate person with even the faintest trace of literary taste could ever get through more than two pages of it for pleasure that one is astounded and terrified at the thought that seven million Americans have found something in it to hold their attention.[7]

These three different reactions to the same text reflect the bent and preconceptions of the different readers; the book itself becomes almost incidental to what each of the readers brought to it, and what they thereby made of it. And what Wilson's reaction suggests is that as we learn more about the nature of the medium and its potentialities, we may well outgrow a particular medium of communication, or a particular level of presentation within a medium. This need not mean that the medium is totally rejected in favor of a more complex one; in an information-rich society like our own, we may use one medium for one kind of satisfaction and others for different kinds; and we may be able to distinguish, within a single medium, a sufficient variety of content to satisfy a great variety of needs, touch upon a great number of levels of fulfillment, and appeal to a wide range of sensibilities and expectations. The book still remains the medium most capable of adapting effectively to the greatest number of different needs, from the prereader's picture book to the most extended analytical treatment of complex and advanced content. It is seldom the only medium at any of these levels, but it is the only one that is so notably effective at every one of them.

Exposure to any form of communication is like any other kind of educational experience; deeper involvement in it carries a wider range of satisfactions for those who learn from their experience to probe more deeply and more widely into the capacity of the medium to convey different levels of content. What readers bring to the book, viewers to the film, and listeners to the symphony makes a difference in the messages they take from it, and each medium is capable of refinements, nuances, and depths that only repeated experience with the medium can bring to light. Expectation, then, is part of the communication experience; different users of the same medium and even of the same substantive message may well take away quite different meanings or effects: a useful fact, or a surge of deep emotion; stimulation or indifference; reinforcement or challenge; immediate reward or long-term influence. There are those who read *Moby Dick* to learn about the whaling industry in the nineteenth century or who take away from a serious film on a contemporary social problem only the how-to information on current fashions in clothes, speech, or courtship behavior. How and why people use the communications they receive is as important an influence on a communication's effectiveness as the intent of the communicator and the nature of the message.

The Range of Communication Experiences

IT IS IMPORTANT, TOO, TO RECOGNIZE THAT A GROWING sophistication in interpreting one kind of communication can have reciprocal effects on the use of other communication formats. One of the unforeseen findings of the earliest studies of readers, which is continually reinforced by later and current studies, is the fact that the people who do a lot of reading ("good readers") are not—as tradition had once pictured them—loners, bookworms, or people who shut the door against the hurly-burly of the "Real World" to lose themselves in the unreal world of fantasy and impracticality. Over and over again, the surveys show that the people who read books also read newspapers and magazines, and they participate more widely in a variety of nonreading activities as well. They attend concerts, listen to lectures, watch television, go to the movies, see plays, take part in political and social activities, engage in sports, and assume leadership in community affairs. They are the ones most frequently identified as "opinion leaders" — the "Communication Elite" in the N-Step Flow of Information — who carry the messages of print to those who themselves cannot read, or who do not even though they can. The image of the reader-as-recluse is true only for a few of the constant readers; the life of the mind is not tied — anymore, if it ever was — to a single channel of communication.

It is interesting to note, in contemporary writing, how frequently the allusions go beyond the literary ones to "quotations" from other art forms. In a quick and dirty survey I once did of my own reading of the next ten novels that came to my hand, I found that allusions to movie actors, directors, dialogue, and even stylistic tricks of the camera were as much in evidence as, in the literature of the past, were allusions to Scripture, myth, or other written "classics" with which it was once taken for granted that the reader would be familiar. In today's society, it may well be true that simply to be literate — even highly literate — is not enough. One must be *adept at receiving messages,* a skill that includes traditional literacy but goes considerably beyond the traditional limits implied by the etymological roots of that term, which would tie it to letters.

There are, however, built-in characteristics in each medium that may militate against their communication effectiveness for some people. If one is color-blind or tone deaf, certain kinds of communication experience cannot be received, however eager one may be to get the messages. The responsibilities of the communicator — the person with a message to send — include the need to recognize the limitations, for some part of the intended audience, of the medium chosen. In these cases, if a wider or more varied audience is sought, the sender must introduce appropriate additional, or alternative, symbols. Thus there are translations, and popularizations, and closed-caption telecasting.

This phenomenon of multiple coding is so ubiquitous that most of us are unaware of its challenge to our own communication practices, although good communicators are called upon daily to resort to it. In so simple a communication as traffic signals, for example, red, yellow, and green lights carry their messages even to the illiterate, but red and green are not readily distinguishable to those who are color-blind. To correct for that communication problem, an additional coded message was introduced: if red is always at the top and green at the bottom, *position* can be read as a coded message by those for whom color does not serve the purpose. A more recent example of the communicators' sensitivity to the different capabilities of different audiences is the user-friendly vocabulary introduced when the computer became small enough and inexpensive enough to seek a wider group of nonspecialist users. Whether the motivation is humanitarian, financial, or educational, the sender of a message must bear in mind that the receiver is an essential part of the communication transaction.

A poet may be content to lose all those readers who do not respond to the devices of poetry, but other communicators have a responsibility to make sure that the message they send will be received and understood by all those who have need of it. The librarian, for example, cannot be indifferent to the many different levels of need for information, and libraries attempt to provide a great number of guides, signals, signs, and variously encoded messages of interpretation and direction to supplement their personal services of information retrieval. To the extent, however, that the finding device is filled with professional terms known only to the librarian ("For holdings, see main entry"), it is the library, and not the patron, who has failed in the communication exchange.

In a sense, this capacity to anticipate the special needs of the receiver, and so encode the message as to remove distorting "noise," is related to style and manner in the composition of a work of art. It is sometimes difficult to recognize any affinity between the composition of public announcements (This Way Out) and the creation of poetry (Something there is . . .), but in each case there is the element of choice of symbol and the ordering of the parts that characterizes all effective communication. The kind of effect being sought and *the kind of receiver for whom it is intended* alter the kind of selection to be imposed.

The preferences of the receivers affect their response to the medium as well as to the message it carries. There are those who are more moved by the visual image than by the written word, even though they are proficient in the use of both. In one of my class assignments, I used Shirley Jackson's short story "The Lottery" and the film made of it, controlling the use so that half of the class read the story before seeing the film, while the other half saw the film before reading the story. I then asked them to analyze which they found the most effective in creating its special mood and emotional impact. My hypothesis had been that the tendency would be to like best the one that was experienced first, but this turned out not to be true. The analyses clearly reflected a preference for the particular sensory experience as such. Regardless of the order in which the students came upon the two versions, those who preferred the printed story spoke of the superior power of the word and those who preferred the film, of the superior power of the visual image. What we have here may be an example of the influence of the right and left sides of the brain upon personal preferences and capabilities. However we explain it, the experiment illustrates once again that what one brings to a communication experience will influence what one takes from it. Each of the formats (print or film) was effective for its audience; no absolute "better" or "less-good" judgment can be made about the presentations without consideration of the question: "for whom?"

It is very difficult for those to whom a particular form of communication is effective to recognize that all others may not be able to share the experience, even when they may share with us the same language and the same level of literacy. In Anthony Powell's work *The Valley of Bones*, the narrator, present when a fellow officer has experienced a personal and career disappointment, tries to express his empathy by quoting a literary allusion that strikes him as particularly apt. He gets no sign of interest or awareness from his colleague. "I was impressed for the ten thousandth time," says the narrator, "by the fact that literature illuminates life only for those to whom books are a necessity. Books are unconvertible assets, to be passed on only to those who possess them already."[8]

Samuel Vaughan has made something of the same point: "The book can reach finally only the literate—and of those, only the ready, willing, and able."[9] Yet we know that many people who are not constant readers can be moved by a reading experience that has relevance for them. When it will be relevant, what is the proper moment for the experience to take hold, is controlled as much by the reader's readiness as it is by the desire of the writer. The point is that simple literacy does not a reader make and that the communication experience is a shared one only when both the receiver as well as the sender are able to carry out the obligations of their roles in the exchange.

Thus when we concentrate on the *books* that made a difference we are limiting our universe not just to people who can read but to people for whom reading has a special significance. Had the question been "What communication experience made the greatest difference in your life," the answers might well have identified such nonreading experiences as a classroom lecture, a sermon, a film, a play, or a musical performance. I used to do a kind of Sabine survey as a standard exercise in my class in communication, exploring any "reading" experience (not just that of reading a book), and even that small an extension widened the range of responses considerably. Right up there, along with the Bible, Aristotle, and other predictable citations, one student listed "the catalog of the library school," for example. Hardly a "Great Book," but nevertheless a reading experience that influenced his choice of a career field and led to an outlook that held throughout the rest of his professional life, in a way that no accepted classic of literature or philosophy could so literally have done. A stop sign on the highway or a skull-and-crossbones label on a bottle is likely to have saved more lives than any critically acclaimed work of literature.

On the other hand, a much more subtle, qualitative difference, not visible to the naked eye or the individual insight, may well have been overlooked by most of the respondents, both in the Sabine study and in my classes' responses. The student who recognizes that seeing Nureyev perform made him a lifelong devotee of ballet thereafter may not ever perceive that certain other attitudes may have been planted by such unidentifiable influences as the comfort and warmth of grandpa's lap, forever after associated with the children's book read to him in those circumstances. Or, at the other extreme, he may not realize that the emotional impact of a hated class assignment, resisted at the time, was never forgotten — precisely because of the turbulent feelings it aroused — and eventually made a connection of lasting importance.

All too frequently the study of effects has been hampered by the assumption that an effect takes place immediately and can be measured at the time that the communication is received. This is often the basis for a judgment on the effects of the mass media. A total series of projected programs may be canceled if the reception of the first one or two telecasts is not immediately enthusiastic. That there can be a delayed reaction, or a step-by-step development of interest, or a matter of simple timing of the program in relation to many other seemingly irrelevant events is not taken into account.

The problem of the delayed or unrecognized impact is one of the most difficult aspects of identifying and measuring communication effects: those to whom they happen, the people to whom we would logically go for our data, simply do not know. The effects are often delayed, and the decisive information may have been stored away below consciousness, to be conjured up when needed with no remembrance whatsoever of the source from which it came. More importantly, many of the effects of any communication may be cumulative rather than dramatically apparent at once. Wilbur Schramm has suggested that the effects of communication may best be likened to the development of a stalagmite: while no one drop of liquid creates the stalagmite, each drop is affected by the ones that went before and then affects all those that come after. The final structure cannot be attributed to any single drop, yet every single drop had an effect, and had any one of them been different, the end creation would have been altered.[10]

Thus any communication experience may have an effect, even the ones we no longer remember. Each one may help prepare for what comes next, open our minds to receive ideas for which we might otherwise not be ready, or, conversely, a communication experience may give us the one argument too many that thereafter turns us off from every other one like it.

Another weakness in many studies of communication effects is the assumption that "effect" is synonymous with a change in the direction of one's thinking: a "difference" in its most familiar sense of "unlike," rather than in its sense of "significant." Effects of communications are not measured only by the ideas that *changed* our minds; there are also ideas that reinforce beliefs already held, and there are probably more instances of these than the road-to-Damascus flashes of insight that make more dramatic copy. It would be wrong to assume that an experience that confirmed us in a belief is not as important as one that turned us in a different direction. To know more surely, to feel more secure in one's position, to find affirmation rather than reversal, to be better armed to fend off opposing ideas—these are not unimportant results of reading or any other communication experience.

Nor are the effects always in the direction intended by the sender of the message, as was the assumption underlying the Bullet-to-Target theory. Students of communication effects have a separate category for this "Boomerang Effect," which turns us in the direction opposite from that advocated in the argument. (Some hard-sell pitches so irritate the recipients that they stop buying the product, irrespective of how well the product performs its function: "I've read so much about the bad effects of smoking that I've decided to give up reading.") And there are communication experiences that have completely irrelevant effects: the measurable impact of the film version of *For Whom the Bell Tolls* was not on public opinion about the war in Spain; it was in the introduction of Ingrid Bergman's closely cropped hairdo, which turned up on women's heads across the country after the film's release. In instance after instance we see the phenomenon repeated: the receiver of the message is often a more potent influence on its effects than is the sender of it.

Despite all that we have learned about the effects of communication, it is still not possible to predict with much accuracy how any given message will affect those it reaches — particularly if we are more concerned about each individual receiver than with the overall general reception by a large, undifferentiated "audience." Certainly the study of effectiveness of different forms of encoding and transmitting messages that will affect the receivers of them has been pursued with all the resources for research at their command by the experts on advertising and mass persuasion. Yet while some expensive and imaginative advertising campaigns have been highly successful, some — equally expensive and imaginative — have not. The same box score for communication success or failure can be cited for well-written books and poorly written ones; films that were meant to be blockbusters and those that turned out to be sleepers; telecasts and radio shows and operas and plays and paintings and statues and ballets and comic strips and presidential campaign speeches and sermons and billboards and bumper stickers and tee shirts. You win some and you lose some, no matter how wise a sender you are.

The proliferation of messages continues. All of us are constantly inundated with messages — some of vital importance, some with no real content to impart, some of relevance to only a small part of the audience they reach. And so the reader or viewer or listener selects, screens, reacts consciously, or is touched subliminally, and only rarely can he tell the interviewer whether a specific experience made a difference or not. Many of the Sabines' respondents were able to identify such an experience, but who knows how many other experiences had an effect that they did not recognize or remember? We should be very skeptical when respondents tell us that no single communication experience has ever made an important difference to them.

Even more difficult for respondents would be the task of identifying the indirect influences, in which the argument that affected them came at second or third hand, in a conversation in which an unidentified quotation had a relevance, even out of context, which at the time was only taken in but not yet processed for its future use. The N-Step Flow of Information cuts across many different communication channels, affecting the individual receiver and being affected by him or her. In trying to measure or evaluate the effects of communication, researchers have tended to concentrate primarily on the medium and have paid, perhaps, far too little attention to the role of the mediator.

Implications for Libraries

THIS OBSERVATION HAS TWO IMPORTANT IMPLICATIONS for libraries and librarians as part of the communication chain. A local public library, for example, is frequently the mediator that makes it possible for the original message to reach—across time and space and social class – the individuals in the community. Thus the role of the librarian-as-selector – the gatekeeper function – has an influence on the community, of which few people, including librarians, are ever aware.

Equally interesting is the probability that the influential people to whom others turn for advice and discussion, the ones who exert that personal influence identified in the N-Step Flow theory and who turn up as the important factor at the moment of decision-making, are very likely to be library users. If the library's users are the Communication Elites (that is, people, regardless of their social or economic class, who are open to many sources of information and who are sought by others to be, themselves, sources of information), then they carry the message to many more people than ever appear in the circulation records of the library. The messages contained in library materials can, through the N-Step-Flow process, reach many people who never set foot in the library.

This suggests that libraries exercise a far greater reach indirectly than can ever be reflected in their annual reports. Whom we reach in this manner, how we reach them, and how they reach others are questions that have not been explored, and may not be explorable by any of the methods and devices now available to us.

This does point up something, however, about the importance of preserving the record. The significance of preserving a record of our thoughts and discoveries has recently been played down, and even rejected, by many in the communication field, including some librarians themselves. The stress upon currency, the urge to discard the book (or any other medium of communication) that has not been used a lot *lately,* and the equation of numbers of users with the value of the experience are typical of the present time. Immediacy, speed of transmission, and number of copies have become the approved measuring sticks.

But the individual experience is still of concern to librarians, who know that a book that is out-of-print is not necessarily a book that is no longer of value, and that whether an idea is new and exciting to a person need have no relation to when it was first expressed, whether it is widely popular, or whether many other people (who may even have been untouched by it) came upon it long before. The realization that the individual experience is just as important, just as valuable, and just as deserving of attention as the mass experience and that its value is not necessarily without broader social importance simply because it is not simultaneously shared by many others reflects a contribution made almost exclusively by the library and the librarian. The library is dedicated to the need and interest of each individual separately, rather than to a faceless mass audience in a given place at a given time. The concept of information retrieval is widely recognized, but retrieval may involve a search that cuts across time, and it is not limited simply to the identification of the latest item of "current awareness."

Conclusion

WHEN ONE THINKS FOR EVEN A MOMENT ABOUT HOW complex the encoding, transmission, reception, and assimilation of ideas can be, the everyday processes that make for effective communication become something little short of a miracle. Messages come through to us from such a variety of sources, in such a variety of formats, through such a variety of obstacles, and with so little formal awareness on our parts as we take them in and use them, store them, and call them up later (often transformed by us in ways that make their original format unrecognizable) that their identification and measurement probably require another miracle.

In the following passage, Richard Stern describes the experience of a twentieth-century American, somewhere on an island off the coast of Maine, listening to the radio transmission of a recording of a Beethoven quartet:

> Notes the dropsical, bilious deaf man had inked a century and a half ago on score paper were stroked on catgut by four men, agitated the air, made electric pulsings, scratches on oiled platters. And how many other losings and findings till the content of that ear-blocked, in-turned head in Austria became the inside of another one on this land dribble of the American coast. Instead of a mess, there was something lit and lucid. Connection. A handshake of the species across years, languages, space.[11]

"Something lit and lucid," "Connection," "A handshake of the species across years, languages, space." In a word: Communication.

As readers of this passage, we come to a deeper understanding of the experience of listening to music, but we have come to it through a similarly complex process of another kind: words the contemporary man tapped out a few years ago on typing paper were reset in type, bound in boards, and filed by some system for retrieval on the shelves of a home or library. And how many other losings and findings till the miracle of musical composition, interpretation, and translation into performance became the inside of our heads wherever we may be, however far away from either Austria or the American coast.

As we read this passage of Stern's, we become involved in the wonder of musical communication, yet the experience of listening to music is quite unlike the experience of reading printed words. Through his mastery over the code of print, Stern enables us to share the musical experience, which depends on another code that is indecipherable to many of us. The losings and findings — what you and I do with what Richard Stern has done with what engineers have done with what musicians have done with what Beethoven has done — represent a miracle that we experience daily in uncounted ways through the many media of communication.

The Sabine survey has told us a great deal about reading and some of its effects, but it is only a single step in the complex study of a far broader world of communications and their effects. We still have a lot to learn and understand about a phenomenon that touches and changes us daily in very complex ways but is seldom consciously noticed because of its very dailiness. Reading, and reading limited to books, is a major part of that phenomenon, but it is not all of it.

In our attempts in the future to learn more about the effectiveness of communication, it will be essential that we pay equal attention to all the elements in the communication process: the sender, the channel, the code — and the receiver. There are still frontiers to explore and unknown continents to map in the realm of experiences that make a difference in our lives.

NOTES

1. One of the most successful projects sponsored by the Center for the Book has been the survey *Books That Made the Difference,* for which Patricia and Gordon Sabine interviewed all manner of people all across the United States, asking just two questions: "What book made the greatest difference in your life?" and "What was the difference?" Gordon and Patricia Sabine, *Books That Made the Difference: What People Told Us,* Library Professional Publications (Hamden, Conn.: The Shoe String Press, 1983).

2. There are a sizable number of people who are interested in the book because it is handsomely bound, beautifully illustrated, or sufficiently rare in its particular format to be fondled, protected, and displayed in locked cases, but not necessarily read. The Sabines' concern, however, is really with the *reading* experience, and whether the reading was done in paperback, hard cover, or first edition does not matter.

   It is true, of course, that in certain cases the total book, and not just its verbal text, is part of the total message. The Tenniel illustrations in *Alice,* and Maurice Sendak's illustrations for his books are undoubtedly an inseparable part of the "reading" experience in those instances. By and large, the respondents to the Sabines were speaking about the printed, verbal content rather than the object that contained it. This essay explores a wider definition of *communication* precisely because any single communication format may well call upon more than one interpretive skill to obtain the full value of its message.

3. Paul Lazarsfeld, Bernard Berelson, and Hazel Gaudet, *The People's Choice* (New York: Columbia University Press, 1948).

4. Claude E. Shannon and Warren Weaver, *The Mathematical Theory of Communication* (Urbana: University of Illinois Press, 1949).

5. Harold D. Lasswell, "The Structure and Function of Communication in Society," in Lyman Bryson, ed., *The Communication of Ideas: A Series of Addresses,* Religion and Civilization Series (New York: Harper and Brothers, 1948), p. 37.

6. Andrew M. Greeley, "An Introduction to *The Robe,*" in Lloyd C. Douglas, *The Robe* (Boston: Houghton, Mifflin Company, 1986), p. xvii.

7. Edmund Wilson, " 'You Can't Do This to Me,' Shrilled Celia," in his *Classics and Commercials: A Literary Chronicle of the Forties* (New York: Farrar, Straus and Company, 1950), p. 206.

8. Anthony Powell, *The Valley of Bones* (Boston: Little, Brown, 1964), pp. 233-34.

9. Samuel S. Vaughan, *Medium Rare: A Look at the Book and Its People,* R.R. Bowker Memorial Lectures, New Series, no. 4 (New York: R.R. Bowker Company, 1977), p. 13.

10. Wilbur Schramm, "The Effects of Mass Communications: A Review," *Journalism Quarterly* 26 (December 1949), p. 397.

11. Richard Stern, *Natural Shocks* (New York: Coward McCann and Geoghegan, Inc., 1978), p. 255.

COLOPHON

Type	Open Capitals and Berkeley
Composition	Acorn Press, Rockville, Maryland, and General Typographers, Washington, D.C.
Cover paper	Strathmore Grandee, Valencia Red
Text paper	Mohawk Superfine, softwhite, smooth finish
Printing	Bruce Printing Inc., Cheverly, Maryland
Foil stamping	Raff Embossing, Washington, D.C.
Illustration	Rudolph Ruzicka, 1930
Design	John Michael, Rockville, Maryland